EXPLORING OUR UNIVERSE

THE SUN

HEATHER C. HUDAK

Checkerboard Library

An Imprint of Abdo Publishing
abdopublishing.com

abdopublishing.com

Published by Abdo Publishing, a division of ABDO, PO Box 398166, Minneapolis, Minnesota 55439. Copyright ©2017 by Abdo Consulting Group, Inc. International copyrights reserved in all countries. No part of this book may be reproduced in any form without written permission from the publisher. Checkerboard Library™ is a trademark and logo of Abdo Publishing.

Printed in the United States of America, North Mankato, Minnesota

102016
012017

THIS BOOK CONTAINS RECYCLED MATERIALS

Design: Emily O'Malley, Mighty Media, Inc.
Production: Mighty Media, Inc.
Editor: Paige Polinsky
Cover Photograph: NASA
Interior Photographs: Getty Images, pp. 21, 23; Mighty Media, Inc., p. 11; NASA, pp. 7, 8, 15, 19, 24, 27, 29; Shutterstock, pp. 5, 12, 13, 17, 18; Wikimedia Commons, pp. 20, 21

Publisher's Cataloging-in-Publication Data

Names: Hudak, Heather C., author.
Title: The sun / by Heather C. Hudak.
Description: Minneapolis, MN : Abdo Publishing, 2017. | Series: Exploring our universe | Includes bibliographical references and index.
Identifiers: LCCN 2016944826 | ISBN 9781680784091 (lib. bdg.) | ISBN 9781680797626 (ebook)
Subjects: LCSH: Sun--Juvenile literature.
Classification: DDC 523.7--dc23
LC record available at http://lccn.loc.gov/2016944826

CONTENTS

	Mission: Exploring the Sun	4
Chapter 1	From Beginning to End	6
Chapter 2	Journey Inside the Sun	10
Chapter 3	Light and Life	12
Chapter 4	Spots, Flares, Winds	14
Chapter 5	A History of Discovery	16
Chapter 6	Saved by Gravity	22
Chapter 7	Solar Studies	26
	Solar Guidebook	28
	Glossary	30
	Websites	31
	Index	32

MISSION
EXPLORING THE SUN

Have you ever played outside on a summer day? You likely felt the sun's warm rays on your skin. The sun is the biggest, brightest object in our **galaxy**. It brings heat, light, and energy to Earth. Without the sun, there would be no life here. Our planet would be too cold and icy.

Super Star

The sun is actually a star. It's the closest star to Earth in the universe. But it is still very far away. Imagine there is a highway leading straight to the sun. It would take more than 163 years to drive there! Earth's next closest star is 250,000 times farther away than the sun.

Milky Way Marvel

Most stars are part of large clusters called galaxies. And there are billions of galaxies in the universe. The sun

Earth's atmosphere bends light. So, we can still see the sun after it has disappeared over the horizon.

belongs to the Milky Way **galaxy**. The sun spins on its axis as it orbits the center of the Milky Way.

Stuck in the Middle

The sun is at the center of our solar system. This giant ball of light makes up more than 99.8 percent of our solar system's mass. It is about 109 times larger than Earth.

CHAPTER 1

FROM BEGINNING TO END

To watch the sun's birth, you would need to travel more than 4.5 billion years back in time. That is when our solar system formed. The sun began as a huge cloud of gas and dust particles. Energy waves pressed the particles together. Gravity made them spin and collapse inward.

As the cloud compressed further, it spun faster. Over time, it became a flat, pancake-like disk. Leftover chunks of gas and dust orbited the disk. These eventually became our solar system's eight planets.

Most of the disk's mass clumped at its **core**. Its temperature became hotter and hotter. Finally, a **protostar** formed. Over the next 50 million years, this protostar's core continued to collapse. It also became much hotter. Eventually, it grew into the star we call the sun.

This stellar nursery, or nebula, contains more than 300 newborn stars.

The force of gravity is very strong in the sun's **core**. It fuses **hydrogen** atoms together, creating **helium**. This process, called nuclear fusion, makes a lot of energy.

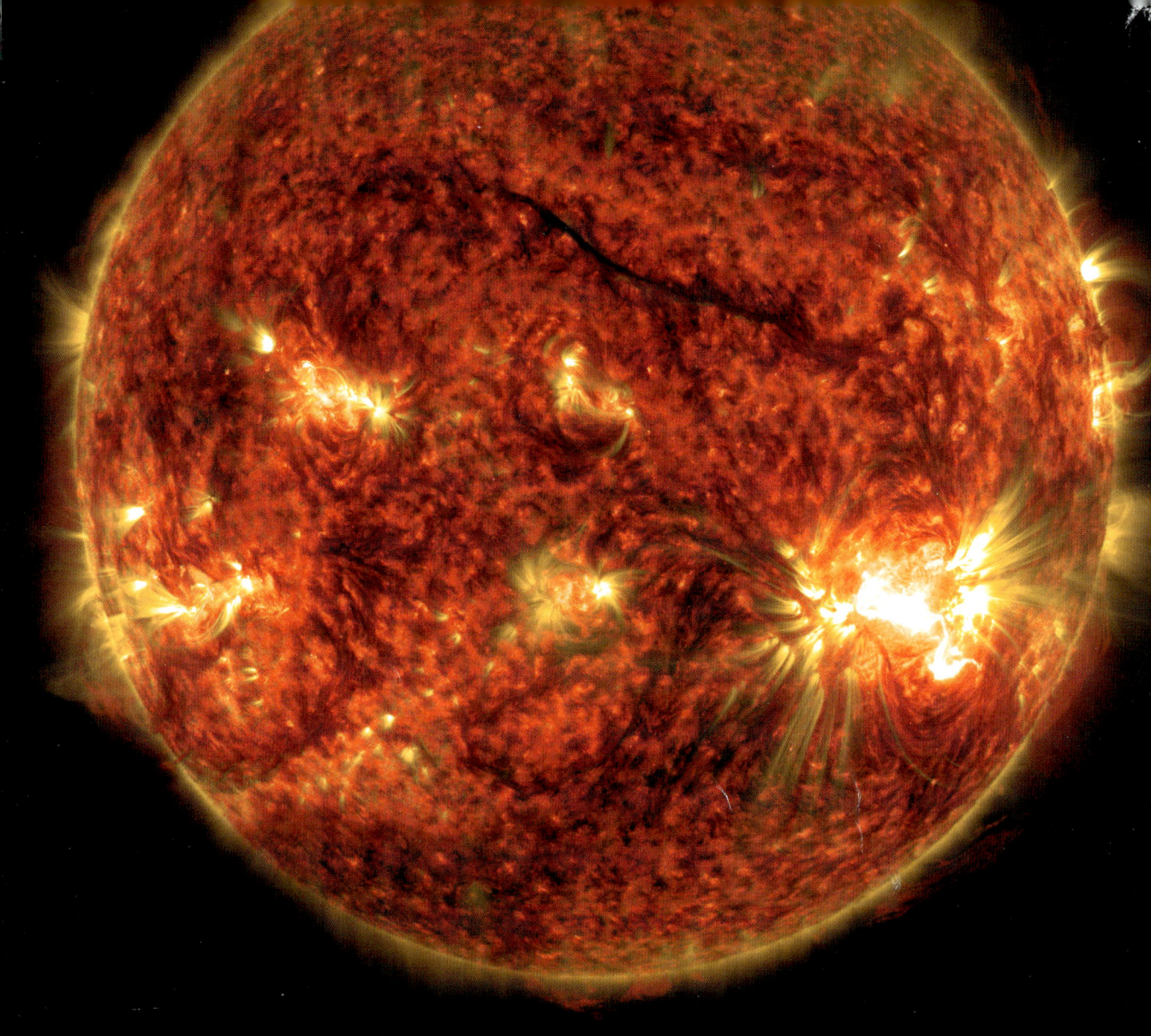

The sun has burned about half of the hydrogen in its core. This means it is halfway through its life cycle.

RUNNING OUT OF TIME

Today, the sun is a big ball of glowing, hot gases. These gases are about 70 percent **hydrogen**. **Helium** accounts for another 28 percent. The remaining 2 percent is **nitrogen**, carbon, oxygen, and other gases. Nuclear fusion is constantly changing hydrogen into helium. This process makes the sun glow.

Eventually, the sun will use up all of its hydrogen. The sun will then begin to die. When nuclear fusion stops, the sun's **core** will start to collapse. It will grow much larger and much hotter. In fact, its heat will make life on Earth impossible.

Over time, the sun will begin to shrink. It will spend **trillions** of years cooling down. In its final stages of life, it will go completely dark.

DID YOU KNOW?

Scientists believe the sun will start to die about 5 billion years from now.

CHAPTER 2

JOURNEY INSIDE THE SUN

The sun has many layers, like an onion. Each layer has a different temperature. And every layer is extremely hot!

The sun's innermost layer is the **core**. The core makes up about 25 percent of its mass. It produces the sun's energy. This energy grows cooler as it moves outward. First, it moves to the radiative zone. It takes about 1 million years to break out of this zone.

Next, energy travels to the convective zone. This is the sun's final inner layer. After energy passes through this zone, it reaches the photosphere. This is the lowest layer of the sun's atmosphere. Sunlight, the light we see on Earth, comes from the photosphere.

DID YOU KNOW?

It takes 150,000 years for energy to travel from the sun's core to its corona.

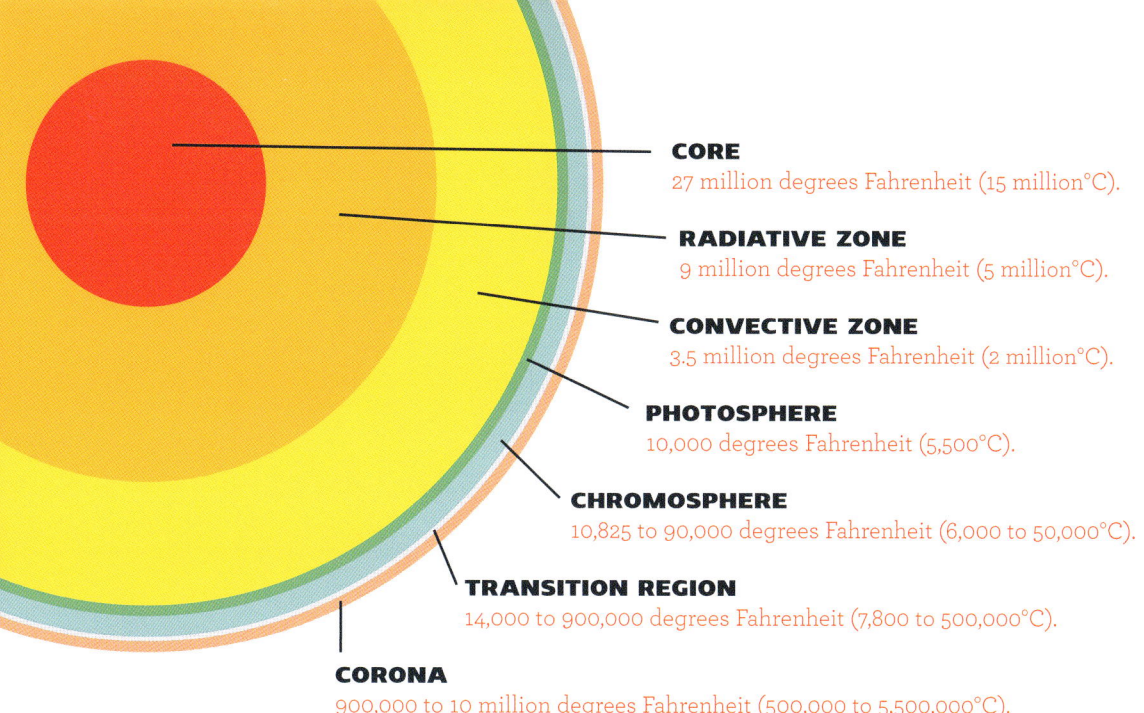

CORE
27 million degrees Fahrenheit (15 million°C).

RADIATIVE ZONE
9 million degrees Fahrenheit (5 million°C).

CONVECTIVE ZONE
3.5 million degrees Fahrenheit (2 million°C).

PHOTOSPHERE
10,000 degrees Fahrenheit (5,500°C).

CHROMOSPHERE
10,825 to 90,000 degrees Fahrenheit (6,000 to 50,000°C).

TRANSITION REGION
14,000 to 900,000 degrees Fahrenheit (7,800 to 500,000°C).

CORONA
900,000 to 10 million degrees Fahrenheit (500,000 to 5,500,000°C).

The next atmospheric layer is the chromosphere. The chromosphere emits red light that cannot be seen by the naked eye. Scientists use special telescopes to view it.

After the chromosphere comes the transition region. Here, the temperature leaps from about 14,000 to 900,000 degrees Fahrenheit (7,800 to 500,000°C). But that's nothing compared to the sun's outer layer, the corona. Temperatures there can reach 10 million degrees Fahrenheit (5.5 million°C)!

CHAPTER 3

LIGHT AND LIFE

Imagine a world without the sun. In this place, the sky is always dark. Oceans are frozen. Plants wither and die. Plant-eating animals have no food to eat. As they disappear, so do the animals that rely on them for food.

The sun's **core** releases energy. This energy travels 93 million miles (150 million km) to Earth. It makes the journey at a speed of 186,000 miles per second (299,338 kms). This is the speed of light.

Solar panels turn sunlight into electricity. Many homes and business now use solar energy.

Plants use the sun's energy to grow. This process is called photosynthesis.

Once the sun's energy reaches Earth, it's used in many ways. Much of this energy is stored underground in **fossil fuels**. Humans burn these fossil fuels to release the energy stored within. They use this energy to power cars and lights, heat homes, cook food, and more.

DID YOU KNOW?

It takes 8 minutes and 20 seconds for the sun's energy to reach Earth.

CHAPTER 4

SPOTS, FLARES, WINDS

The sun is an ever-changing ball of activity. Sometimes its **magnetic field** explodes. Energy particles and clouds of **plasma** shoot into space. This creates sunspots, solar flares, solar winds, and other solar activity.

Sunspots are found in the sun's photosphere. These spots look dark because they have a lower temperature than the surrounding areas. Solar flares are bright bursts caused by huge explosions of the sun's magnetic field. They often occur with coronal mass ejections (CME). These are large plasma eruptions.

Some solar activity can reach as far as Earth. This is called space weather. Solar wind carries space weather to Earth and throughout the solar system. It is made up of plasma that shoots out of the sun at a speed of 1 million miles per hour (1.6 million kmh).

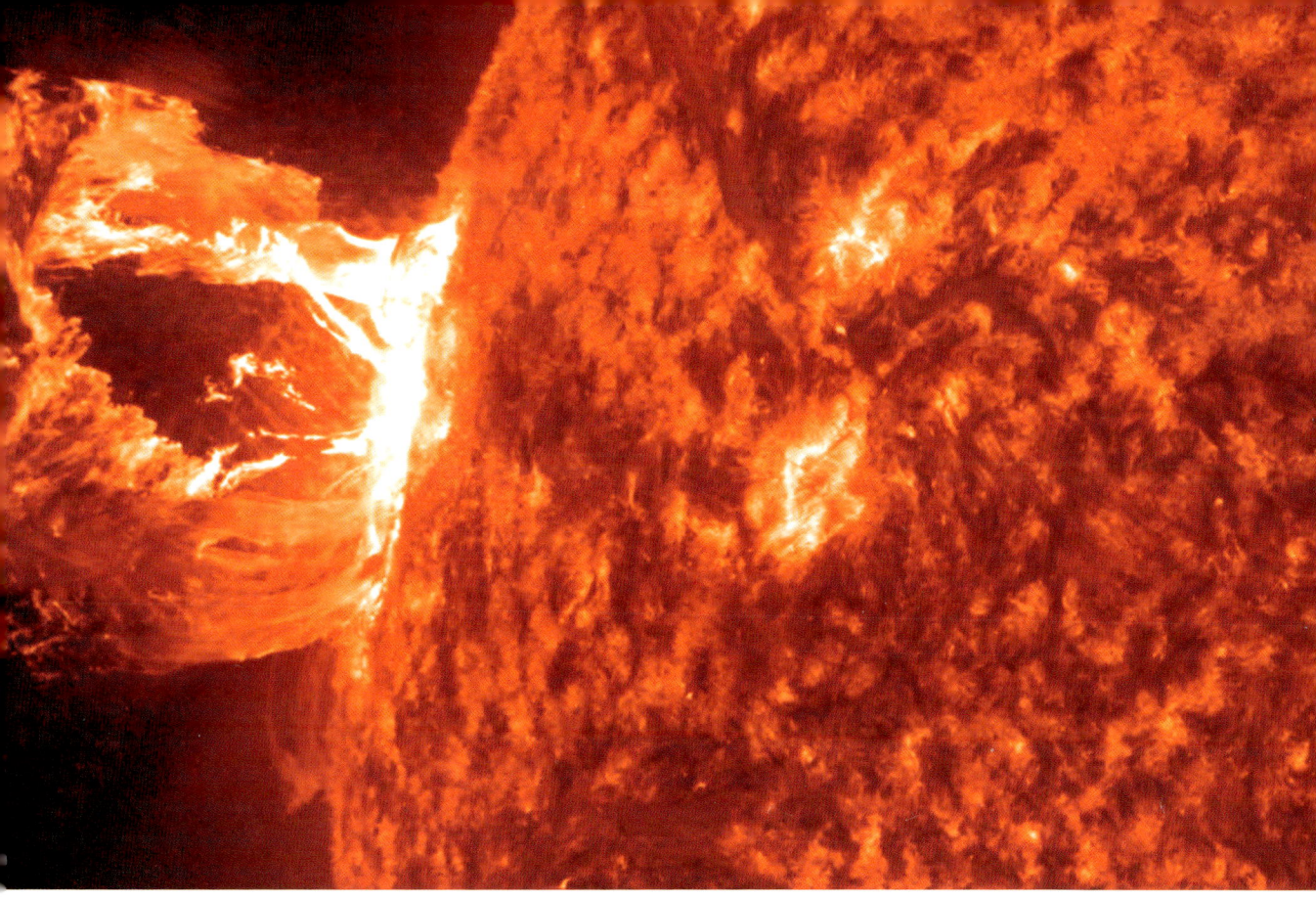

A CME shoots from the side of the sun. If the CME pointed toward Earth, it could cause errors in navigation devices.

Solar wind takes about three days to reach Earth. Sometimes it causes power failures. It can also interrupt communication systems. About every 11 years, solar activity reaches its peak. It then begins a new **cycle**.

CHAPTER 5
A HISTORY OF DISCOVERY

The sun has amazed people since the dawn of time. Ancient **cultures** observed its movements through the sky. They watched it rise and set in the same positions each day. This pattern was used to track time. It was also used to track the seasons.

Early humans tried to explain the sun. Ancient Greek, Egyptian, and Roman myths describe a sun god. His carriage carried the sun across the sky each day. The **Aztec** people worshipped their own sun god. They believed he fought a dark force. If he lost, the world would end.

Some ancient buildings were built with the sun in mind. The city of Petra, Jordan, was designed so the sun would light its sacred places. Many **Mayan** temples and Egyptian pyramids **align** with the sun's position in the sky. This happens at certain times of day and on religious holidays.

Petra's monastery was built about 2,300 years ago.

17

Attempts to understand the sun led astronomers to begin mapping stars and planets. In the 100s CE, Egyptian astronomer Ptolemy believed Earth was the center of the universe. The sun and planets orbited around it.

Ptolemy's theory was later disproved. In 1543, Polish astronomer Nicolaus Copernicus claimed the planets orbit the sun. In the 200s BCE, Greek astronomer Aristarchus had made the same claim. But it was not well supported. Copernicus faced a similar challenge.

In 1609, an Italian astronomer changed the way people saw space. Galileo Galilei supported Copernicus's theory. Using a telescope, Galileo proved that the planets orbit the sun.

A statue of Copernicus holding a model of the Earth and sun

Eight planets orbit the sun. Mercury is the closest. It is only about 36 million miles (58 million km) from the sun.

German scientist Johannes Kepler improved Copernicus's theory. He also studied the sun's interaction with the planets. His theories were called the laws of planetary motion.

DID YOU KNOW?

The first telescope was made by a Dutch eyeglass company. Galileo was the first person to study the sky with this new tool.

Kepler's first law proves the sun is at the center of the solar system. It also says the planets move in **elliptical** orbits. Kepler's other laws state that the planets do not orbit the sun at constant speeds. This explains why planets move faster when they are closer to the sun.

Kepler paved the way for English scientist Sir Isaac Newton's studies. Newton invented the reflecting telescope in 1671. It helped him look much deeper into space. He used his findings to further explain Kepler's three laws. He also discovered the law of gravity. This had a huge impact on science.

Newton's reflecting telescope was the first of its kind.

SUPER SCIENTIST

SIR ISAAC NEWTON

Sir Isaac Newton was born in England in 1642. From a young age, Newton was very interested in mechanics. As an adult, he studied math, light, and colors. In the 1680s, Newton began writing his own theories.

In 1687, Newton published a book that explained his thoughts on motion and gravity. His ideas had never been heard before. The book became one of the most important in the history of science. Newton's thoughts on gravity helped people understand how planets orbit the sun.

According to legend, an apple fell on Newton's head while he sat beneath a tree. This inspired his theory of gravity.

CHAPTER 6

SAVED BY GRAVITY

What keeps the sun, moon, and planets from crashing into each other? Gravity! Gravity is a force that attracts objects to each other. All objects have a gravitational pull. But the strength of an object's pull depends on its mass. An object with a larger mass has a stronger pull.

The Earth has great mass. It pulls many things toward it, including people, oceans, and the moon. The sun is the largest object in our solar system. This makes its gravitational pull the strongest. Everything is pulled toward it, including the planets. So why don't they fall into the sun and burn?

Force of gravity also depends on distance. An object's pull is stronger when it is closer to another object. Each planet moves forward on an **elliptical** path. The sun's gravity pulls the planet inward, but the planet's elliptical

Without gravity, we would fall off Earth and float in space. Astronauts experience this floating sensation when they travel far enough from Earth.

path pulls it away. This constant battle keeps the planet in orbit. It also explains why Earth is close enough to the sun to support life, but far enough away that it doesn't burn.

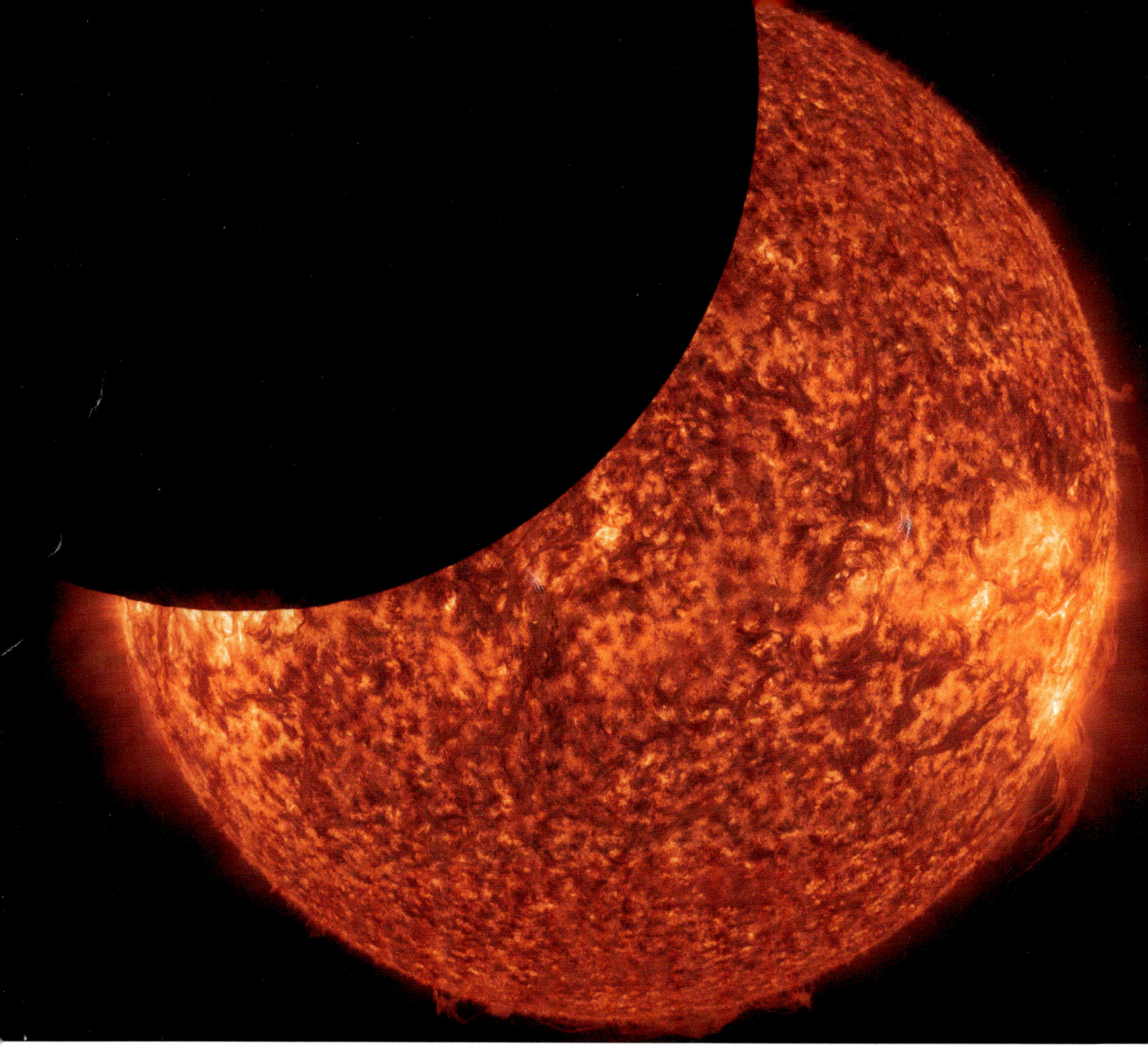

On January 30, 2014, a partial solar eclipse lasted two and a half hours. This is the longest ever recorded.

Earth's temperature depends on its distance from the sun. In the summer, Earth tilts toward the sun. There are more daylight hours and the weather is warmer. In the winter, Earth tilts away from the sun. The days seem shorter and the weather is colder.

An equinox happens when Earth tilts equally toward and away from the sun. There are two equinoxes each year. The vernal equinox is the first day of spring. The autumnal equinox is the first day of fall. On these days, there are an equal number of daylight and nighttime hours.

OUT OF SIGHT

Sometimes the sun disappears briefly during daylight hours. This is called an eclipse. Eclipses happen when at least three celestial objects **align**. A solar eclipse occurs when the moon comes between Earth and the sun. The moon blocks the sun from view. And the sun's light casts a shadow of the moon on Earth.

CHAPTER 7

SOLAR STUDIES

The sun is too bright for us to look at it directly. And it is too hot for us to visit. Instead, we must use telescopes and spacecraft to study the sun. The first solar spacecraft were called Orbiting Solar **Observatories** (OSO). In the 1960s and 1970s, eight OSO **satellites** were launched. They collected data from a single 11-year solar **cycle**.

Scientists later studied the sun's relationship with Earth. The National Aeronautics and Space Administration (**NASA**) launched the Solar Terrestrial Relations Observatory in 2006. Scientists use its data to create detailed digital images of the sun.

We have learned a great deal about the sun. But there is still more to learn. And we are always looking for new ways to explore our sky's largest star. Many more missions are planned to help achieve this goal in the future.

TOOLS OF DISCOVERY

SOHO

The Solar and Heliospheric Observatory (SOHO) was built by NASA and the European Space Agency (ESA). NASA launched SOHO in 1995. The spacecraft was designed to collect data on the sun's structure and atmosphere. It was originally meant to operate for two years. But it was so successful that it is still in orbit today!

SOHO continues to study the sun. It also helps scientists keep an eye on space weather. Photos from SOHO are often posted on the Internet for the world to see.

ESA engineers carefully observe SOHO's assembly.

SOLAR GUIDEBOOK

Age
- 4.5 billion years

Other Names
- Sol or Helios, after the Roman and Greek gods of the sun

Type of Star
- Yellow dwarf

Elements
- 70 percent **hydrogen**, 28 percent **helium**, 2 percent **nitrogen**, carbon, oxygen, and other trace gases

Size
- 870,000 miles (1.4 million km) in **diameter**

DID YOU KNOW?
The largest recorded sunspot occurred on April 8, 1947. The spot was more than 35 times larger than Earth.

Distance from Earth
- 93 million miles (150 million km)

Rotation
- 25 to 36 Earth days

Speed of Orbit
- 450,000 miles per hour (720,000 kmh)

Surface Temperature
- 10,000 degrees Fahrenheit (5,500°C)

Hottest Temperature
- 27 million degrees Fahrenheit (15 million°C) at the core

On June 20, 2015, the Solar Dynamics Observatory spacecraft took its 100-millionth photo of the sun.

GLOSSARY

align — to be in line with something.

Aztec — a people who ruled a large empire in present-day Mexico in the 1400s and early 1500s.

core — the central part of a celestial body, usually having different physical properties from the surrounding parts.

cycle — a period of time or a complete process that repeats itself.

culture — the customs, arts, and tools of a nation or a people at a certain time. Something related to culture is cultural.

diameter — the distance across the middle of an object, such as a circle.

elliptical — shaped like a flat oval.

fossil fuel — a fuel formed in the earth from the remains of plants or animals. Coal, oil, and natural gas are fossil fuels.

galaxy — a very large group of stars and planets.

helium — a light, colorless gas that does not burn.

hydrogen — a gas with no smell or color that is lighter than air and catches fire easily.

magnetic field — the region around a magnet or an electric current in which the magnetic forces can be detected.

Mayan — of or relating to an ancient Indian people who lived in Central America and Mexico from about AD 250 to 900.

NASA — National Aeronautics and Space Administration. NASA is a US government agency that manages the nation's space program and conducts flight research.

nitrogen — a colorless, odorless, tasteless gas. It is the most plentiful element in Earth's atmosphere and is found in all living matter.

observatory — a place or a building for observing the weather or the stars.

plasma — a substance that is similar to a gas but that can carry electricity.

protostar — a cloud of gas and dust in space believed to develop into a star.

satellite — a manufactured object that orbits Earth. It relays scientific information back to Earth.

trillion — the number 1,000,000,000,000, or one thousand billion.

WEBSITES

To learn more about Exploring Our Universe, visit booklinks.abdopublishing.com. These links are routinely monitored and updated to provide the most current information available.

INDEX

A
Aristarchus, 18

C
Copernicus, Nicolaus, 18, 19
coronal mass ejections (CME), 14

E
Egyptian pyramids, 16
equinoxes, 25
European Space Agency (ESA), 27

F
fossil fuels, 13

G
galaxies, 4, 5
    Milky Way, 4, 5
Galilei, Galileo, 18
gravity, 6, 7, 20, 21, 22, 23

K
Kepler, Johannes, 19, 20

L
laws of planetary motion, 19, 20
layers, 10, 11, 12, 14
    chromosphere, 11
    convective zone, 10
    core, 7, 9, 10, 12
    corona, 11, 14
    photosphere, 10, 14
    radiative zone, 10
    transition region, 11

M
magnetic field, 14
Mayan temples, 16

N
NASA, 26, 27
Newton, Sir Isaac, 20, 21
nuclear fusion, 7, 9

O
Orbiting Solar Observatories (OSO), 26

P
Petra, Jordan, 16
planets, 4, 5, 6, 9, 10, 12, 13, 14, 15, 18, 19, 20, 21, 22, 23, 26
plasma, 14
protostars, 6
Ptolemy, 18

R
religious holidays, 16

S
Solar and Heliospheric Observatory (SOHO), 27
solar eclipses, 25
solar flares, 14
Solar Terrestrial Relations Observatory, 26
solar wind, 14, 15
space weather, 14, 27
sun gods, 16
sunspots, 14

T
telescopes, 11, 18, 20, 26